THE MAINE HOUSE II

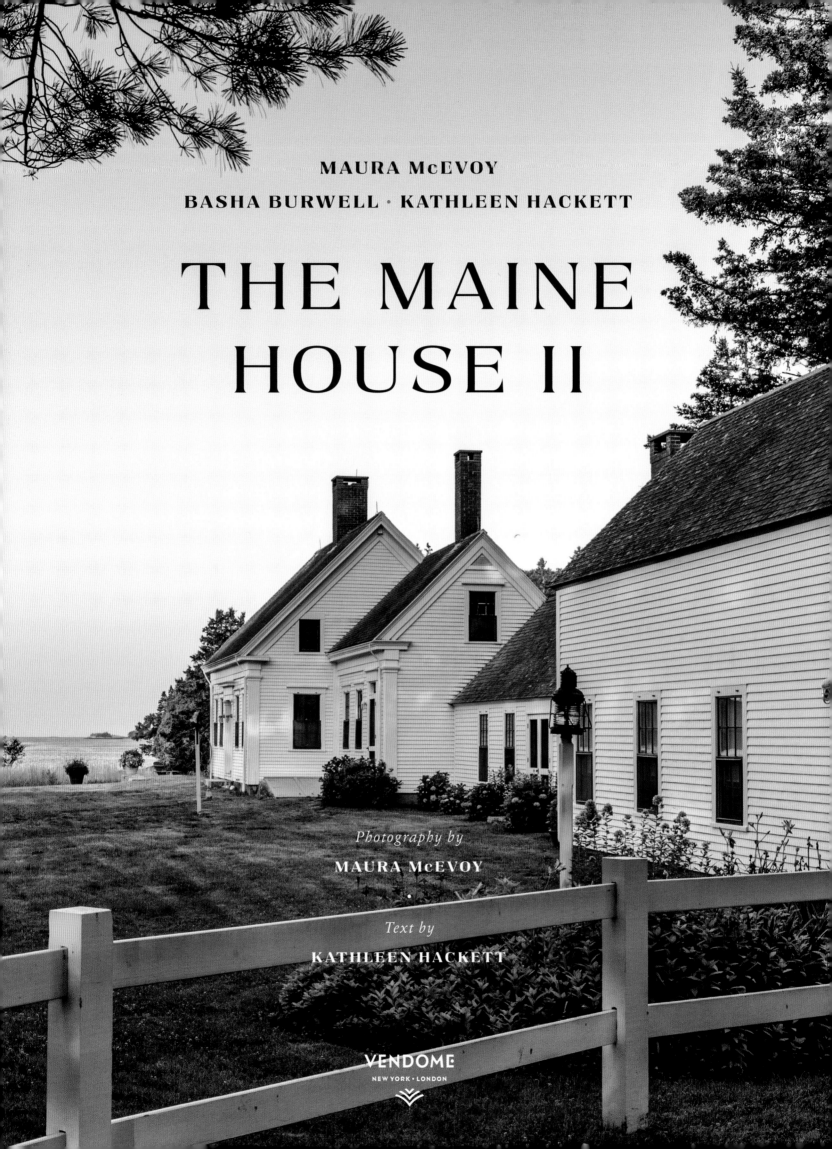

MAURA McEVOY

BASHA BURWELL · KATHLEEN HACKETT

THE MAINE
HOUSE II

Photography by

MAURA McEVOY

·

Text by

KATHLEEN HACKETT

VENDOME

NEW YORK · LONDON

CONTENTS

INTRODUCTION

"Are we being good ancestors?"

·

In five simple words, virologist and medical researcher Jonas Salk, who developed the first polio vaccine in 1955 (and declined a patent because he felt it should be held "by the people"), asks a question both potent and poignant. And though Salk's inquiry relates to science and medicine, the sentiment is universal. In fact, his question followed us throughout our Maine travels: down rural roads, over mountains, around lakes and ponds, out to islands and through fields and forests, as we spent the last three years in search of (more) houses that exemplify what makes a house a *Maine* house.

We set off on an optimistic note. Our first book, *The Maine House*, expressed our desire to record the Maine of our childhoods, a Maine that is swiftly vanishing. The book sounded a rallying cry, one that journalist Heather Chapman so perfectly summed up as crafting

---

Lobster boats point into the wind as the sun goes
down on Monhegan Island's harbor.

"... a plea to preserve a living history belonging to individual, family and state; a visual call to recognize these homey structures and others like them as extraordinary gifts. [The authors] have gone into these old homes and salvaged something we'd do well to hold on to: the understanding that when the last cottage is crumbled and family farmhouse flattened, so goes the unrenewable character and charm that is uniquely Maine."

Precisely.

As it turns out, we found kindred spirits everywhere. The reception to our first volume was astonishing, confirming what the three of us have long known to be true: that Maine casts a spell unlike anywhere else in the world. It is what artist Jamie Wyeth means when he says, "I could live four lifetimes and not scratch the surface of what this place exudes." Spend any amount of time here—a weekend, a summer, a lifetime—and it gets under your skin and streams through your consciousness forever. We were humbled by the outpouring of thanks and admiration for what we had created; what began as a passion project became a point of connection with people all over the world. And the message was loud and clear: we are not alone in our conviction.

If *The Maine House* was our cri de coeur, this second volume represents a mission, one that aims to illustrate that it is possible, indeed essential, to rescue Maine's quirky architectural history if we are going to preserve its singular nature, one that goes hand in hand with a reverence for the land. To that end, we set our sights not only on houses that have been preserved, renovated, restored, rescued, and sensitively expanded but, equally as important, on the people who live in them. When we walked into the 175-year-old home of Tom and Mary Ann Young (pages 114–25), for example, and spied a pull

––––––––

OPPOSITE: No carving your initials here! Faded postcards, miniature paintings, and newspaper clippings create a Delft-like wallcovering in an outhouse in the woods.

quote torn from a newspaper taped to the window casing that reads, "Old buildings can be used," we knew we were in the right place. The minute Ben Emory (pages 76–83) mentioned that he refused to cut down the stately tamarack that blocks his view of the ocean, we felt awe. And relief. The sheer determination of Joe Cutts to keep his off-the-grid family home (pages 194–203) from succumbing to both the elements and modern conveniences inspired us like no other. And nothing was more charming than when Jack Partridge (pages 234–47) showed us the list—dutifully carried in his chest pocket—of possible upgrades (dishwasher, bidet, mattresses) to the century-old island cottage where the family agreed to install electricity only in 2001. It is a sentiment that Basha summed up when she arrived at her family cottage (pages 22–31) this past summer to find that the coverlet she had known for a half century had been replaced. "There was a familiarity that was so comforting. And that won't come back for fifty more years." When the owner of a handsome cottage that has been in the family for almost seventy years (pages 32–43) shared with us that she might paint away the decades-old, high-contrast green doors in a butter-yellow room, the three of us weighed in: pull one thread, and the whole thing can unravel.

Change, of course, is inevitable. And as the sensitive addition that architect Jocie Dickson designed for her family's lakeside camp (pages 150–59) demonstrates, it can complement, rather than erase, the past. Change of use, too, wields this same power—and taps into an ethos that seems to permeate Maine's salt-and-pine air: "Here, we use what we have." When the Bright family grew too large to fit under one roof, they turned a boat shed just steps from the shoreline into a summer cottage that is the stuff of dreams (pages 204–11).

———

OPPOSITE: Formerly a farmer's pigpen, then a coal-storage bin, the diminutive building, now one of the most enchanting cottages on the Midcoast, was moved to this island ledge in the late nineteenth century.

The Colonial Revival where John Fondas and John Knott spend their summers is no longer the hotel built for Gilded Age rusticators, but it looks like it could be, so meticulous is the exterior renovation. Inside, the linoleum runner, EXIT signs, and myriad original doors (and their room numbers) remain (pages 212–25). There is beauty and dignity in largely leaving things as they are. And, perhaps, nowhere is that more compelling an idea than in the lighthouse where Jamie Wyeth lives through all four seasons (pages 274–93).

We are proud—and so very grateful—to have the opportunity to create a second visual record of this special place. Our hope is that it at once enchants, transports, inspires, and deepens the resolve to take care of what one acquaintance in our travels calls a "thin place," derived from the Celtic phrase *caol ait*, in which the boundary between heaven and earth is, yes, thin. The following pages are filled with houses whose owners can proudly answer Salk with a resounding "yes." It is a question worth asking ourselves no matter where we are. Because, as the decorated scientist concluded, "If we want to be good ancestors, we should show future generations how we coped with an age of great change and great crises."

·

Maura McEvoy
WELLS, MAINE

Basha Burwell
BROOKLIN, MAINE

Kathleen Hackett
ROCKPORT, MAINE

———

OPPOSITE: Crane your neck just so and you might spot the arriving ferry through the porthole window in the Partridge family's island cottage (see pages 234–47).

INSHORE

Basha Burwell

THE COTTAGE

. . .

Good chaos. That's how I love to think of this place—the last remaining original cottage on this beautiful Midcoast harbor—which has defined seven generations of family. It was built in 1910 by my Uncle Bill's grandfather, artist William Harden Foster, who Uncle Bill thinks came here on a grouse-hunting trip. Maybe with his friend L. L. Bean? Or maybe to stay in the grand hotel that once stood on these shores. Uncle Bill loves to reminisce about the drives to Maine from Connecticut every summer. Especially the time his sister packed her pet chicken, Gloria, into the boat they were trailering because it was the only place the caged bird would fit.

Little has changed since the first few generations gathered here—same chairs, same beds, same aluminum lobster plates, same sit-up clawfoot tub, largely reserved for adults, because what kid needs a bath when there is an ocean out front to swim in? I have slept in the same bedroom here since I was young. Its weathered walls, the triptych of photographs of my grandmother and grandfather on their beloved picnic boat, *The Whistler*, the country curtains, the creaky bedsprings, the awkward lamps that require a backup flashlight for stealth reading, the sliver of a view—all still the same. The youngest generation still piles into the "playhouse," the tiny outbuilding that Uncle Bill's cousin Janet, on the Monro side of the family, started as a summer school for neighborhood kids when she was seven. She ran it for seventeen years, because the Cottage is a place where you can count on things. The family numbers more than fifty now, and to this day we gather on the front porch at five o'clock, where the adults sip cocktails and everyone devours saltines with my grandmother's famous hot crab dip.

But it is the lobster pot that Uncle Bill's mother kept by the front steps, in front of a squeaky webbed lawn chair, that tells the story of the Cottage the best. She filled it to

---

The village gathering place for decades, the front porch is alive from sunup to sundown, serving as the summer living room, dining room, and reading room.

the brim with peroxide and water, the best solution for soaking the inevitable stubbed toes that accompany a barefoot Maine summer. Every kid in the village used that old soaking pot, since the Cottage was the neighborhood hangout. My grandmother welcomed *everyone*, and now my Aunt Mary does the same. Sleepovers, games of sardines, sack races—the Cottage abounds with children and laughter and the occasional tear every summer. Uncle Bill loves to tell the story of the time his mother was doing her nightly bed check and found plenty of kids sleeping—none of them hers. But that's the thing about this place. It draws you in and holds on in a way only family can. There may be many more of us now, yet little has changed. More happy voices on the porch and at the annual clambake. More memories. More love. This place will always be my ballast, my anchor, my compass. Because there is no better feeling than being a part of something. And the Cottage? It is *something*.

ABOVE: Change has come to this harbor village, but the view of the river
and islands beyond has remained the same for more than a century.
OPPOSITE: Yankee ingenuity at work: why bother with a wood
bin when a Mission chair does the job just as well?

OPPOSITE: A stillness pervades the hallway, and yet the
walls, floors, and ceilings have absorbed the laughter, tears,
and joys of this sprawling family for generations.

ABOVE: A nautical map of Casco Bay fit perfectly
between the door jambs, so that's where it went.

OVERLEAF: The kitchen is stocked with only the essentials,
including two lobster pots and a hammer—hanging from a
nail in a handy spot—for cracking hard-shell lobsters.

OPPOSITE: Uncle Bill's grand-father once illustrated and wrote articles for Scribner's in the back bedroom, where a working boat model and a constellation of paintings and photos by family and friends line the walls.

•

ABOVE: The Cottage proudly sits on a bluff overlooking one of the prettiest harbors in Maine.

•

RIGHT: Photos and mementos hang over a twin bed in accidental gallery style.

RACE CHART

NORTHEAST HARBOR

LETTERS. 1

LETTERS. 2

BILLS

WATER'S EDGE

...

Most families mark the growth of their children by their ages or their grade in school or by recording it in pencil on a doorjamb. But the seagoing parents of a teenage son chart the years in Maine time. Or more specifically, Maine sailing time. "He's grown up on the water— first as a rower, then as a sailor, and now as a racer," says his dad, whose great-grandfather was the commodore of the nearby yacht club and whose parents met there as college kids.

For this family, Mount Desert Island is as close to heaven as it gets: sailing its sound is their religion; the congregants are a large extended family of grandparents, aunts, uncles, and cousins. Indeed, it was on a foggy day while on a watch boat during a family regatta that the husband's maternal grandmother spied the wood-frame house—or what he affectionately calls "the box on the rocks"—built in 1924 and set close to the shoreline. "A ray of sun broke through and shone directly on the house as if to announce itself to her. She determined its siting to be the best on the island," he says. To be sure, it was on sturdy ground. Water's Edge sits on a towering granite ledge left behind as the last glaciers retreated more than fourteen thousand years ago to form Somes Sound, one of the most breathtaking waterways in Maine.

As if to mark his own birth, the owner's grandparents acquired the place in 1963, the year he was born; he has spent every summer of his life here since. Little has changed at Water's Edge in the last half century—it would be unthinkable to strip the fireplace of its original black paint or swap out the painted faux rug in the dining room for a real one.

———

This is a family bound by their love of sailing; every nook is
filled with nautical antiques and racing ephemera.

"The chairs in there are not the sturdiest, but I have looked forever to replace them, and I just can't," says the wife. Perhaps that's because this family, surrounded as it is by its treasured family history, is too busy making its own. When the grandmother chose this house, she knew it was all about what lay beyond it: as you enter through the front door, there is a view straight through the back door to the water—and out to the beloved boats that have been in the family for generations. "We don't even unpack when we arrive. We run down to the dock and row out to the boats. For us, the water is the ultimate connection—to the place, to the people, and most importantly, to each other."

———

OPPOSITE: There's no need to pass the binoculars in this house; multiple pairs, shelved beneath a watercolor by the owner's grandmother of her husband's racing boat, allow landlubbers an up-close view of the boat traffic on the Sound. Gazes turn upward on clear evenings, when the telescope brings the sky close. ABOVE: The family boats, some sailed over five generations, are moored in front of the cottage.

OVERLEAF: Paintings and sculptures by family and local artists fill the living room. The owner's great-grandfather carved the bald eagle that hangs over the fireplace. A three-hundred-pound wooden block pulley serves as a cocktail table.

ABOVE: Hidden and open storage in the dining room perfectly frame the living room fireplace, painted black by the owner's grandmother.

•

LEFT: Waves carved into each of the built-in corner cabinets in the dining room nod to the seagoing passions of the family.

•

OPPOSITE: The painted "rug" in the dining room has lasted more than most carpets; it turned one hundred in 2024.

OPPOSITE: The simple charms of an amateur painting—especially one of a rocky Maine coastline—are not lost on this family.

ABOVE: Treasures from the sea create a still life on the living room mantel.

RIGHT: Fifty-year-old ostrich ferns flank the entry, where the double front doors offer up a view straight through the house and out to the water.

OVERLEAF: Inspired by Japanese teahouses, the folly on the dock offers up a shady spot for a mid-afternoon cup.

THE RESCUE

...

Not long before Stephen Earle's home became his, there were plans afoot to take the wrecking ball to it—to build a parking lot. The Greek Revival, one of the last with an original attached barn in this coastal village, escaped such a sorry fate thanks to the perseverance of local residents. To demolish it, they argued, would be to lose forever a piece of the town's soul.

Instead, they gained a steward in Earle, a native Michigander whose compass has been pointing toward Maine for the better part of forty years, since his college days in New England and throughout his professional life in New York City. The interior architect and designer, whose reverence for house and home spans fourteen different dwellings into which he has poured his heart and soul, cites the one thing that has remained a constant throughout. "I have been moving five boxes labeled 'For a House in Maine' from one place to the next for the last four decades. I just could never get rid of them."

It was while visiting friends on the Midcoast, where a lobster feast in a house overlooking the harbor brought him straight back to his childhood on Michigan's Upper Peninsula, that Earle felt he had come full circle. Indeed, while he was looking around the house—peeking into rooms papered over in pink flowers with

The depth of Earle's classic big house, little house, back house, and barn is deceptive from the street, as the buildings are attached from front to back.

OPPOSITE: Earle had been carrying around a swatch of this wallpaper, a nineteenth-century pattern, for forty years before he found an ideal space to hang it. ABOVE: An orphaned sconce purchased long ago at a flea market and a mirror bought for a photo shoot: Earle found a place in the house for pieces he had been stashing over a lifetime.

———

plush pink carpet underfoot—the very distracted owner turned to him and said, "I don't know who you are, but the way you are looking at this house, I think you are going to live here." Earle likes to say that if he were turned into a house, it would be this one. "It's like a suit that fits perfectly."

It took some convincing to get his partner, Mitchell Gross, to feel the same. Why own a house an eight-hour drive away? Why not just visit occasionally? But after several visits himself, the born-and-bred New Yorker got it. "He saw just how *of* this place I feel. It's not enough to simply be *in* a place," says Earle. It wasn't just Gross who wondered whether it made sense. Friends cocked their heads in dismay, every one asking him how often he gets here. Which, for Earle, is beside the point. "I'm here every single day in my mind. This is home with a capital H."

LEFT: How to make a 1930s grisaille painting and an intricately carved coffee table work in a Maine house? Throw a sheet over the sofa and create make-do lighting by clipping a lamp to a vintage floor-lamp stand.

BELOW: Earle had no trouble finding a use for the shallow built-in shelves in the guest bedroom. "It's just a tableau of things that I like," he says of the wooden-box collection and books with compelling covers.

OPPOSITE: "You can't be in Maine and not absorb the idea that reusing and making do is what gives a house its character," says Earle, who committed to using furniture he already had before adding anything new. He acquired the rug in a trade with a neighbor.

OPPOSITE: What was once a dark storage room is now the light-filled primary bedroom, where Earle added built-in closets under the eaves for just the right amount of storage. ABOVE: Earle plucked the 1840s painted-pine chest of drawers made in Maine out of storage and returned it to its home.

OVERLEAF: The floors throughout the house were a mishmash of colors and in various states of wear; painting them white was a quick fix. Though he intended to eventually use Maine-appropriate colors, Earle found the white envelope too seductive to give up.

OPPOSITE, CLOCKWISE FROM TOP LEFT: Village residents prevailed in their bid to rescue the
historic home from demolition. Earle added windows to the tiny back house, once a storage room that
is now a light-filled office. The kitchen was the only room in the house that was entirely reimagined.
ABOVE: The dining room pendant is symbolic of the use-what-you-have approach Earle
took to the interiors: he drilled a hole in a gilded wall plaque to make a canopy, hung a 1960s
globe light from an old chain, then surrounded it with a basket-turned-lampshade.

THE FALLS AT CROCKETT COVE

. . .

"It never occurred to me that I had no training in architecture or engineering, nor did I even know anything about building materials. As far as I was concerned, there was wood, stone, and old brick. The more natural the materials the better." Thus wrote Emily Muir in her delightful memoir, *The Time of My Life*. An artist and self-taught architect who designed mid-century homes when she was in her own mid-century, Muir's legacy is bound up in forty-six modest cottages that once dotted a picturesque cove at the tip of one of Maine's storied Down East peninsulas. It is a world away. An environmentalist and philanthropist, the Philadelphia native was instrumental in bringing to the area the esteemed Haystack Mountain School of Crafts, designed by architect Edward Larrabee Barnes. Between them, the pair put down Maine's modernist roots with a shared vision: that every building be a showcase for the landscape.

The Falls at Crockett Cove is among the handful of Muir's cottages that remain. "It had me at the full glass front. But the fact that it sits on a huge piece of granite that hangs out over the water? You can slip into nature without disturbing it," says Carolyn Evans, who together with her husband, Ray, are its current stewards. It is a sentiment that would have Muir, who

---

"Take a rugged piece of nature and build a dwelling to blend in with it (not dominate it). What a challenge!" wrote Emily Muir in her memoir.

OPPOSITE: Local
materials—pink granite,
pine—and glass ease
the transition from
outdoors to in.

LEFT: Muir looked to her
environment for subject
matter and art materials;
a sand mural depicts
iconic Maine subjects.

died in 2003 at the age of ninety-nine, dancing in her grave. "Take a rugged piece of nature and build a dwelling to blend in with it (not dominate it)—what a challenge!" she wrote.

The Evanses' sensitivity is evident everywhere, from the fresh coats of paint matched to the original on the kitchen cabinets to the sheets of the same Formica on the counters to the new flooring chosen to match the old. A pair of back-to-back sofas eliminates choice; they can enjoy the best of Muir by looking out to the view or into the roaring fire.

Such sensitivity to perspective is exactly what Muir was after. "You can just feel her commitment to working with the land, whether you are looking at the house from the water or looking at the water from the house," says Evans. That commitment inspired Evans to the point of devotion: she relented on a long-held insistence on straight lines and left the curved vanity in the bathroom just as it was. "What was important to her is now important to me," she says.

ABOVE: Muir kept rooms intentionally modest, in deference to the sweeping views.

RIGHT: Though Muir's designs were strictly for the warmer months, she knew that every Maine cottage needs a fireplace. The bigger, the better.

OPPOSITE: The architect was less fond of cooking and cleaning than she was of the outdoors and designed her houses to reflect that mindset. Evans left the kitchen largely intact, repainting the cabinets in their original colors and replacing the Formica with a faithful match.

OVERLEAF: Fishnets stretched between the uprights of the deck railings in Muir's designs, so Evans found the closest thing to them—a metal mesh that provides for a relaxing (and safer!) intake of the view.

Kathleen Hackett

BABY M

. . .

We admired it from the street for almost two decades; our morning walks out to the point began here, at one of the last remaining Capes on the harbor. We marveled at its charms every single time, as if noticing them anew: the double hollyhocks that overshot the roofline; the black-green shutters with their anchor motif, a kitschy flourish that seemed just right here; the chunky center chimney that gives the tiny place dignity; the sweet second front door that opens into the kitchen. There was a time when chamber music and the unmistakable scent of oil paint floated through the salt air here, when visiting musicians and artists took up residence in the modest cottages and fishermen's shacks that once dotted this stretch of coastal bliss.

When the place became ours, the neighbors were circumspect. In a village that was in the midst of unprecedented change, further erasure of its past would not come as a surprise, though the sting would last forever. We couldn't turn back time, but maybe this artist and writer could preserve a small piece of the street's storied past.

We were determined to leave the house—built in 1860 and added on to willy-nilly—just the way it was. Aren't those quirks what attracted us to it in the first place? My sister, who lives around the corner, immediately gave it a name: the letter M, the first initial of the street it is on. Apart from removing the dropped kitchen ceiling and cladding our newfound cubic feet in pine planks, we resisted the impulse to expand. Sure, a dormer on the second floor would open things up, but then we wouldn't get to laugh uproariously

---

It's the same ritual every year: lilacs and alliums in bloom mean
it's time to plant the urns with an exuberant mix of rosemary,
strawberries, chocolate cosmos, and water hyssop.

OPPOSITE: Family cameos on cardboard line the wall just inside the Dutch door, which stays open all summer long. ABOVE: The harbor provides: lobstermen and boaters float side by side in one of the few remaining working harbors on the coast.

————

when Stephen's curls—some of the last remaining on his head—graze the eave in the bedroom. Or connect with our sons, Finn and James, each of whom stands on either side of six feet, when we all crowd onto the living room sofa and it feels like Thanksgiving. Admittedly, I am prone to a desire to expand the kitchen, using my work as a cookbook writer as rationale, but then I remember how much I love the daily ritual of flinging open the Dutch door while the coffee brews, then sitting down in the fussy floral chintz chair and sipping it in silence as the sun comes up.

Of course, we did make our mark, largely with buckets of paint, a floor sander, and furniture and art we had collected over two decades. The garden pays homage to the artist who came before us, with luck on our side some years more than others. Still, we tend to both it and the house as if we are merely its caretakers. Indeed, it's not unlike having a newborn: we coddle it, protect it, and never ever want it to grow up.

OPPOSITE: Humor is a common thread throughout: a ship
painting resting on a ledge over the fireplace requires a double
take to realize that it's on fire. And the only way to work a
lobster into the mix was Dalí style, on the landline.

ABOVE: Nothing new here: a mix of vintage furniture, paintings, and
lighting add up to an idiosyncratic living room with characteristic
Maine house moments—a tilted lampshade and lazy pillows.

OVERLEAF: A plaster version of *The Thinker* presides
over the kitchen, where an outsize madeleine pan
makes a clever backsplash behind the stove.

CLOCKWISE FROM ABOVE LEFT:
A boule-as-pillow sits in the morning
reading chair. A former garage for carriages
is now an art studio, lunchroom, and
guest bedroom in a pinch. An ancestor—
along with a monster lobster claw—greets
visitors on entering the front door.

·

OPPOSITE: On a Queen Anne chest
of drawers, a still life of loyal (basset
hound), sentimental (tiny Keds), comical
(doctored painting), and humble
(amateur seascape) treasures.

ABOVE: The dining room is full of people, including a mannerist sculpture in which the boys once hid candy.

RIGHT: Every small house needs a big painting; a floor-to-ceiling abstract oil of a river in winter hangs on the dining room wall.

OPPOSITE: The spoils from walks along the water and in the woods.

A USONIAN HOUSE

. . .

The Maine Coast Heritage Trust has spent the past fifty years protecting and preserving more than 170,000 acres of land and 330 islands in Maine. As one of its founding members, Ben Emory helped pioneer the widespread use of conservation easements to protect privately held land from development, a profession he chronicles, entwined with his other great love, in his 2018 book, *Sailor for the Wild: On Maine, Conservation and Boats.*

Emory's passion for conservation may explain why he refuses to cut down the tamarack that obstructs the sight line from his house to the water. "I'd rather live with a blocked view than take a tree down," he says. The single-story house, built by Emory's parents while he was serving in Vietnam, is now barely visible from the water, but it wasn't always that way. "It really bothered my mother that it stood out in the early years, until the trees grew up around it," he says.

Emory's life—and life's work—has been shaped by the land- and seascape here, a destiny born out of an intrepid paternal grandmother, whose husband was killed in World War I three days before the Armistice, leaving her with three young boys. She decamped from Baltimore to a farmhouse on the harbor here to raise them. That home remains in the family, but when Emory and his siblings began to have children, their father found the farmhouse to have shrunken. "He delighted in his grandkids, but felt they were even better in a different house," he says. "He built this one for its low maintenance."

———

Emory likes his low-slung home for its low
maintenance and its easy relationship with the land.

76

It was a decade ago that a friend and expert on Frank Lloyd Wright declared the mid-century structure Usonian, the name Wright gave to a group of flat-roofed houses built with native materials that forge a strong visual connection between the interior and exterior. "I would say it is *part* Usonian. Those houses had concrete floors; thank God ours doesn't," says Emory, who converted the attached garage into an insulated living space when his own grandkids came along. They use it all summer, but he relishes it most in the winter, when he spends a night in the house each week, a ritual that distills his life's twin passions into a single glimpse. "I wake up to gorgeous mornings, watching the sun come up over the flat, calm sea, and reflecting on the hillside of winterberry bushes," he says.

ABOVE: As if carved from the room itself, the mid-century dining table and chairs have been here as long as the accordion-screened pass-through window and built-in storage below it.
OPPOSITE: A couple of whales, an anchor, a racing boat, a nor'easter jacket: subtle hints in the entryway just off the driveway suggest what's in store on the water side of the house.

OVERLEAF: The living room is a study in Usonian architecture: lots of natural light, open views on the private side of the house, and native materials.

ABOVE: The home is an ideal place to entertain family, friends, and the community. "But I like it when it is quiet," says Emory.

LEFT: A cantilevered bedside table is original to the house.

OPPOSITE: In the guest room, a built-in chest of drawers is a landing place for sentimental photos and the toy boat Emory bought for his young son, who is now in his late forties.

THE DAVIS FARM

...

Drew Hodges likes to tell the story of the first dinner invitation he and his partner, Peter Kukielski, received while trying to decide if life on a Midcoast peninsula suited them. "We were terrified because it was getting dark, and dinner was in the middle of the woods," says Hodges. On their arrival, the host carried a giant wok from an open fire to a table covered in newspaper and flipped it over. "Dozens and dozens of mussels cooked in white wine and butter," he says.

Art lured Hodges, a trained artist and award-winning designer best known for his iconic branding of Broadway shows, to the coast of Maine several decades ago. "While everyone around me was gushing over modern art, I was looking at the paintings of Rackstraw Downes," he says, referring to the British-born artist who painted Maine landscapes in the mid-1960s. But it was that dinner—and the rare saltwater farm that dates to 1826 that he now calls home—that all but captured his soul. "The house recalls Andrew Wyeth's *Weatherside*, which, of course, made it hard for me to turn away," says Hodges. For Kukielski, a former curator at the New York Botanical Garden (where the rose 'Peter's Joy' was named for him) and an expert on disease resistance and sustainability in rose gardens, it was an opportunity to test hardier, pesticide-free roses—and replace the lawn with more sustainable creeping thyme.

———

A shingled dock house sits in perfect
proportion to the land and sea.

The light and landscape continue to captivate them, but it is life around the cove that anchors Hodges and Kukielski here. "There was a whole life waiting for us that we had no idea existed," says Hodges of the friends they have made and the things they have learned how to do, including sailing a boat, practically a requirement when one lives within sight of the water. "I also love that Lois Dodd; N. C., Andrew, and Jamie Wyeth; and Rockwell Kent inhabited this world," he says. But it's perhaps something Kukielski noticed when he first made the trip to Maine that stuck. "He loves to talk about our drives here, especially the part about the toll-booth attendants. He says the closer you get to Maine, the nicer they are."

———

ABOVE: "They're like Monopoly pieces stuck together," says
Hodges of his classic big house, little house, back house, and barn.
OPPOSITE: Hodges was taken with the idea of bringing a digital quality
to the forest, as seen in the quartet of trees that hang in the dining room.

OVERLEAF: The traditional exterior belies what's in store inside.
An exuberant European floor lamp sits in front of a trio of paintings of
Monhegan Island, where Hodges first experienced Maine. "There's a bit
of modernism here. I didn't want it to be a salute to the 1800s," he says.

ABOVE: On a bedroom wall, works
by Maine artists flank *Skowhegan
Woods* by Lois Dodd.

LEFT: Traditional meets contemporary:
a classic door casing frames a pair of
Donald Judd prints that Hodges likes
for their suggestion of horizon lines.

OPPOSITE: Shelves built in right
up to the top of the steep pitch
hold books on the couple's favorite
subjects: art, food, and gardening.

OVERLEAF: Without betraying the house's
essential character, Hodges opened up
what was once a galley kitchen to make
the space friendlier for entertaining.

ABOVE: Kukielski designed walking
paths throughout the property for all,
including goldendoodle Frances, to enjoy.

•

LEFT: The dock house offers a
place for contemplation.

•

OPPOSITE: Hodges brought light into what
was once a dark bedroom by installing a trio
of six-over-six double-hung windows that
mimic the originals found all over the house.

THIS IS BEN'S PLACE

The Boat Landing, "Gurnet," New Meadows River.

PRETTY SOUVENIR ADV. CO., N.Y.C.

We SPECIALIZE IN SEA FOOD

Thank you CALL AGAIN

BEN'S PLACE
Lobsters
Crabs & Clams
ROUTE 24
On The Left Side
Of The Road
GURNET, MAINE

CLOSE COVER FOR SAFETY

VIEW AT

DINNING ROM ENJ
DINNERS GURNET BR

BEN'S PLACE

...

The Coffin family has been lobstering out of the Midcoast since Ben Coffin began setting traps in the early 1900s. Which shouldn't seem all that remarkable, given that Maine is the largest lobstering state in the country. But of its thousands of miles of coastline, just twenty remain accessible to commercial fishermen. It is a statistic that struck Blake Civiello and Lili Liu, whose charming cluster of Monopoly-style buildings perched on a Midcoast causeway is where the Coffins once sold their catch.

The lobster tanks may be gone, but Ben's grandson Clarence, now in his sixties, has been able to keep the family tradition alive, thanks to the civic-mindedness of Civiello and Liu. The couple secured working waterfront status, then allowed the town to set up a clam nursery in their backyard. An oyster co-op, too, enjoys water access here. "It seemed that the property should exist to serve a purpose," says Liu. The couple, whose architecture practice has taken them all over the world, decided to return to Civiello's home state to be closer to family. But by taking on what only architects could— eleven precariously sited buildings in view of all passersby—they got a whole community. The main house, where they now live, was once a café, lobster tanks used to fill what is now a summer kitchen, and locals used to buy clams from what is now the garden shed. "People call it the village, because that's still the feeling here," she

Ephemera dating back to the days when locals knew the cluster of buildings on the causeway as Ben's Place.

says. Perhaps it has something to do with the espresso machine the couple acquired from a shuttered coffee shop. "Fishermen, oystermen, lobstermen, people from town, they all stop into the summer kitchen for an espresso," she says.

Liu, who grew up in Los Angeles, admits she had no idea what she was getting into. Reading Thoreau and E. B. White did not prepare her for the first winter she visited Civiello's family. "I brought my thickest socks and coat. And had to borrow what looked like a duvet with sleeves," she says. Indeed, much of life in the village revolves around responding to the weather. And with it comes physical labor that took Liu by surprise. There are floats to put in and take out of the water every year, firewood to stack, and a lot of doors to attend to: winter doors, screen doors, storm doors. But none of it takes away from what the place gives. "I love the proximity to nature here, how peaceful it is, how I get to see the sunrise. I love the community. I wouldn't have it any other way."

———

ABOVE: The main house, summer kitchen, cottage, bait house, and bridge house
sit on the narrowest strip of land at the foot of a bridge. OPPOSITE: A lobster
pot is as essential to the summer kitchen as a sink and dishwasher.

ABOVE: The couple renovated the formerly uninsulated guest cottage for year-round use.

BELOW: With just enough room for a bed and a small closet, a bedroom tucked under an eave offers a priceless view.

OPPOSITE: Maine's first state flag—the star and pine—makes the perfect window shade.

PRECEDING PAGES: Liu and Civiello
are passionate cooks who, after living
all over the world, travel through
food in their Maine kitchen.

OPPOSITE: Nails driven into the stair
risers make a handy utensil rack.

ABOVE: The former roadside clam
shack is now a garden shed.

RIGHT: The couple is committed to
maintaining their property as a working
waterfront, the number of which are
diminishing up and down the coast.

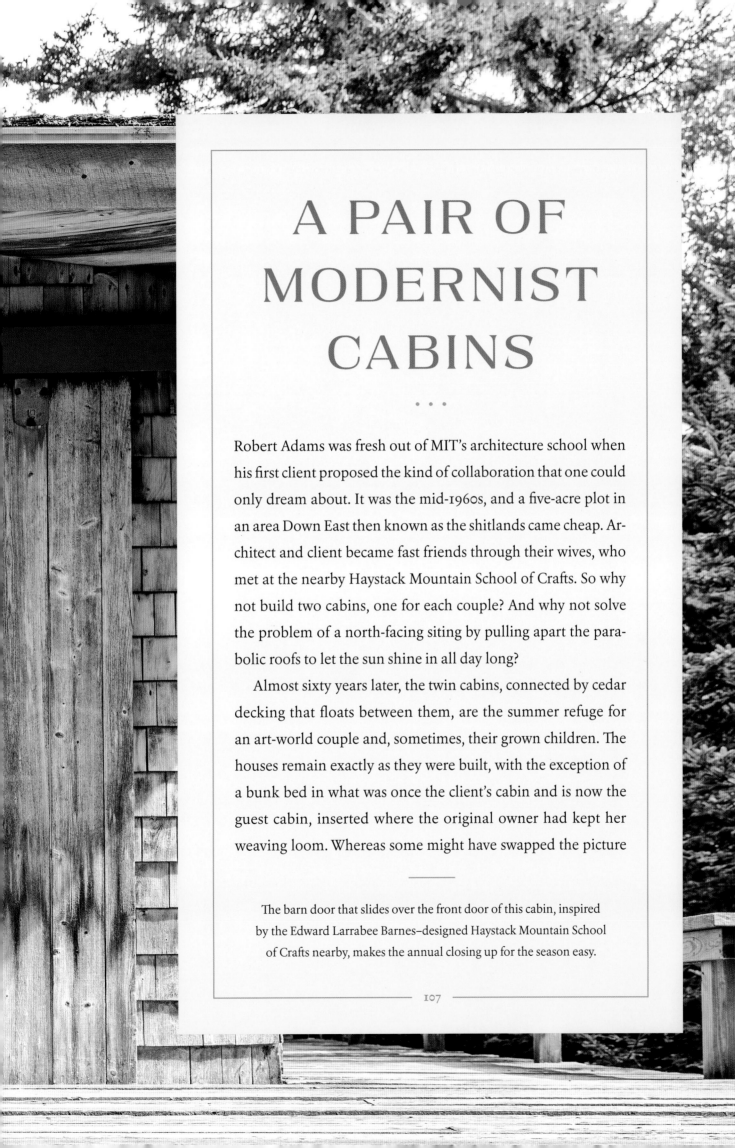

A PAIR OF MODERNIST CABINS

. . .

Robert Adams was fresh out of MIT's architecture school when his first client proposed the kind of collaboration that one could only dream about. It was the mid-1960s, and a five-acre plot in an area Down East then known as the shitlands came cheap. Architect and client became fast friends through their wives, who met at the nearby Haystack Mountain School of Crafts. So why not build two cabins, one for each couple? And why not solve the problem of a north-facing siting by pulling apart the parabolic roofs to let the sun shine in all day long?

Almost sixty years later, the twin cabins, connected by cedar decking that floats between them, are the summer refuge for an art-world couple and, sometimes, their grown children. The houses remain exactly as they were built, with the exception of a bunk bed in what was once the client's cabin and is now the guest cabin, inserted where the original owner had kept her weaving loom. Whereas some might have swapped the picture

---

The barn door that slides over the front door of this cabin, inspired
by the Edward Larrabee Barnes–designed Haystack Mountain School
of Crafts nearby, makes the annual closing up for the season easy.

window facing the woods for the smaller one facing the sea, the couple deferred to the architect's intent. "It turns out that the weaver wanted to be oriented toward the woods. And the cabin does sit up high enough that it feels like a treehouse," says the wife.

As for furnishings, the interiors came together organically. "In the beginning, I announced that one of the cabins was going to be strictly mid-century and the other was going to feature folk-art pieces. My husband just looked at me askance," says the wife. Modernist pieces passed down by the husband's parents and a trove of flea-market finds collected over the years peacefully coexist in both cabins. It would be hard not to in this most idyllic of settings, where the fruits of a long-ago alliance continue to nourish mind, body, and soul. "There are smudges on the ceiling above our bed where the gentlemen who built these cabins pressed the boards into place. I love lying in bed analyzing those fingerprints. They couldn't possibly have known how much peace this place would bring," says the wife.

<hr />

ABOVE: The couple kept the furnishings simple yet simpatico with the period architecture.
OPPOSITE: A fishnet curtain by textile artist John Krynick suggests a separate room
where a bunk bed has replaced the weaving loom stashed there by the original owner.

OPPOSITE: A no-frills galley kitchen
connects the living and sleeping rooms.

ABOVE: The original owners preferred
a view of the woods, so the architect
compensated for the lack of light by
designing clerestory windows above.

LEFT: A simple plaque says it all.

OVERLEAF: A generous deck, where
gatherings happen all summer long,
connects the two modest cabins.

THE HOUSE THAT NOBODY WANTED

. . .

For two decades it was uninhabited, all but ignored, as if, in its decrepitude, it no longer had anything to offer. Houses, like humans, need championing as they grow old, and this Greek Revival, built in 1850 from largely recycled structures, had endured one too many insensitive caretakers. The last one erased its classic proportions by creating a head-scratching warren of tiny rooms, leaving nothing of the original house but the newel post. For the last twenty-five years, Tom and Mary Ann Young, nurturers by nature, have been doing what has long come naturally to them, patiently bringing this quintessential New England home back to life. At the same time, they were raising their two children in a place that had taken their breath away more than thirty years ago. "Our first impression of the Midcoast was while under sail, and we were utterly taken with its majesty. It rises from the coast unlike anywhere else on the Eastern seaboard," says Tom. They felt no urge to sail on.

Ask Young how long it took to restore the orphaned building and he answers the question with a question. "What's today's date?" He likes to joke that his memoir on maintaining a coastal house would be titled *Chasing the Rot*. But it was walking around the village—often noted as one of the prettiest in Maine—that provided him with a priceless archive of architectural details. "I didn't need any new ideas. I just had to look around. They're all right here," he says. With twenty-five restored windows, two symmetrical dormers, a pair of columned porches, yards of siding and trim, and eventually a widow's walk, the house stands proudly amid the understated beauty of its vernacular kin. And it has become the House That Everyone Wants to Be In.

"There's no getting away from the look of a new window," says
Tom Young, who restored all twenty-five of them in the house.
"These are energy efficient and will last a century."

One might guess that this seagoing family would live in polite rooms filled with nautical references. But Mary Ann, an artist with a hungry eye inherited from her flamboyant mother and honed by years of study in textiles and design, has other ideas. In every corner, on every surface, there is an infectious exuberance, sometimes sentimental, often humorous, always off the cuff. Much is informed by family travels by land and sea. "If I like it, I will find a spot for it. Humble or highbrow, it doesn't matter. I love the aha moment," she says. It all dazzles friends and family, who consider the Young house their favorite gathering place. A visiting nephew, at age five, perfectly summed up the joy this home exudes, perhaps taking a page from his Uncle Tom. When Mary Ann asked him what he would like to do, he replied, "I just want to look around."

———

ABOVE: It is a room for cooking, but it perfectly expresses the warmth and generosity that attracts friends and family. OPPOSITE: Tom built the dish cabinet using a pair of found sliding glass doors.

OVERLEAF: Family passions fill the living room, subtly and not so. A pair of carved wooden figures—a sea captain and a fisherman—passed down through Tom's family, is the only nod here to a nautical life.

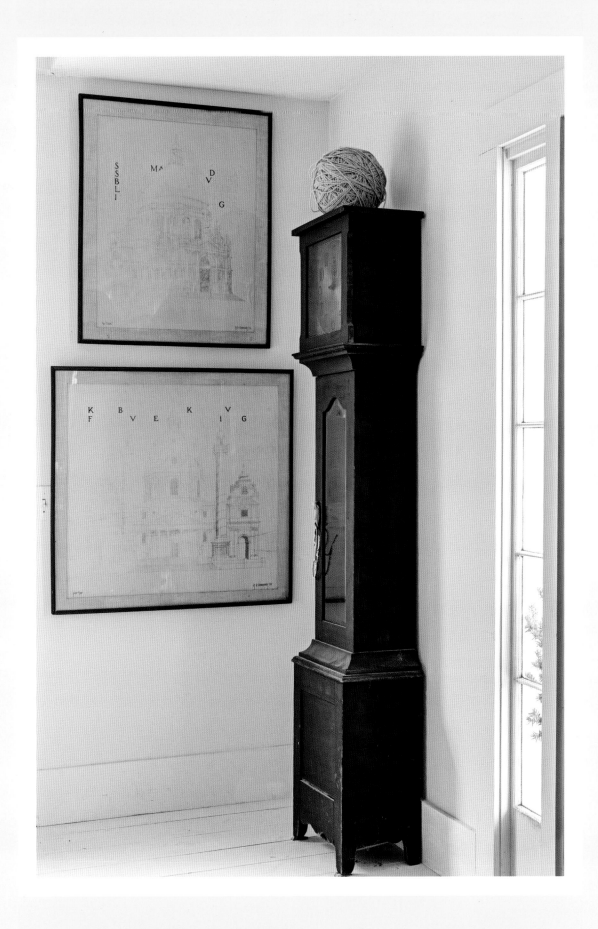

OPPOSITE: A breakfast nook is flooded with morning light. ABOVE: A nineteenth-century grandfather clock reads as sculpture against a crisp white wall at the foot of the stairs.

OVERLEAF: A giant jar of peanuts is a cheeky reference to Mary Ann's nickname, Peanut.

OPPOSITE: Mary Ann hung the weathered buoys, washed ashore and collected over time, from the third-floor ceiling to fill the stairwell.

•

LEFT: Why not stash a Swedish child's chair under an early American table if it fits?

•

BELOW: The newel post was the only original detail remaining in the house when the Youngs became its owners.

INLAND

CLEARWATER

. . .

Every fall, Scott Finlay fills the guest book at Clearwater, the lakeside cottage he and his wife, Martha, spent a full decade restoring, with a synopsis of work completed over the prior year. Seven years ago he wrote, "All the jobs are done." Today Finlay finds this laughable, realizing that houses, especially the seasonal variety, may as well be living, breathing things, as much in need of constant care and attention as newborns. Built in 1910, Clearwater remained in the same family for ninety years, the result of valiant efforts to maintain the property despite few resources and scattered family members. The loss was heartbreaking to them, but in the Finlays, the former owners found a spirit of stewardship and generosity. "They all come back to visit and express their gratitude to us for resurrecting their favorite place in the world from the ashes. They are thrilled that it has been preserved," says Finlay. That is, right down to the taxidermy on the walls and the jelly molds in the drawers. "We're not hunters, but we are careful to honor the tradition of this old camp," he says. Everything that was in the rooms, closets, and drawers remains, including a trim board on the front porch that is marked with children's names and heights.

———

Sunrise on the dock at Clearwater, where the
mailboat will soon arrive to make a deposit into
the box mounted near the front "door."

Such sensitivity to what came before might be traced to Martha's childhood summers spent on a lake in upstate New York. "The only thing Martha ever wanted—besides me—was a house on a lake," says Finlay. A long driveway, worn paths, a stone fireplace, and French doors were on her list too, and Clearwater had them all. "I wanted our two children to have the kind of idyllic summers I had," she says. And in that spirit, the couple has drawn a wider circle that includes artists to whom they loan the cottage for one week every September. An accomplished artist himself, Finlay can pass hours in his barn on woodworking projects. "It is an ideal place to create because you can be completely relaxed. There is no worry about what other people are doing, what they think of you, what you are wearing. One can age gracefully here. It is such an important part of finding peace in our lives," says Finlay.

———

OPPOSITE: The Finlays removed nothing belonging to the previous
owners from the cupboards and cabinets. The Depression glass is marked
with the camp's initials. ABOVE: "Sitting on the porch and taking it
all in is an important part of finding peace in my life," says Scott.

OPPOSITE: Scott likes to joke
with guests that Martha is the
hunter in the family; the couple is
committed to leaving the cottage
just the way they found it, including
the taxidermy and curtains.

·

RIGHT: A Victorian breakfront—
replete with shelves, drawers, nooks,
and cabinets—is an unmistakable
reminder of the camp's history.

·

BELOW: It is as if the furnishings
have grown old with the place;
to add a new piece would attract
too much attention to it.

OPPOSITE: The fun meter, tucked in a corner of the door jamb, is always on max in this house. ABOVE: The Finlays saved as much of the kitchen as possible, including the lower cabinets and drawers, and faithfully reproduced what they couldn't.

OVERLEAF: Scott guesses that fifteen gallons of putty was used to reglaze every single window in the house, each one restored with original weights for opening and closing.

AN ABANDONED CAPE

. . .

Falling in love with a house isn't all that much different from falling in love with a person. Both bring out the optimist in us as well as a kind of benevolence that serves to keep the thrill alive. Flaws? Well, they're charming. There's someone for everyone, goes the old saw, but the agent who represented the aged Cape on a lonely stretch of country road was not so sure. Then she met artists Dan Anselmi and Marc Leavitt. "I remember her saying very clearly, 'Why would you ever want this place?'" says Leavitt. The house, built in 1790, had been abandoned for years, a plus as far as the Boston-based couple was concerned. An orphaned old house is often an architecturally intact house, they reasoned, spared the ersatz renovations and trendy makeovers that would have been inflicted upon it if inhabited. "It was so plain and simple; everything—all of the original moldings, fireplaces, doors, hinges—was there," says Anselmi.

There was no heating system, no family room, no great room, no room for a refrigerator in the kitchen, an ailing roof, and a vertigo-inducing staircase. Anselmi and Leavitt looked straight past all of it, mesmerized by what *was* there. For these two artists, whose professional lives left little time to build their practices and whose Back Bay one-bedroom apartment offered no space in which to do it, it was love at first sight.

Indeed, the pair was so besotted that a full year passed before they realized the house was just a short drive from a bustling Midcoast town. Anselmi and Leavitt commuted from their city apartment every weekend, taking the back route and only stopping for groceries. "We worked like dogs, refinishing walls,

---

A combination of five different paint colors went into the coal-black
exterior of the Cape, which turns a bronze-black in the sunlight.

clearing brush, painting the exterior. We did everything ourselves," says Leavitt. That includes learning a thing or two about country living. "We had to ask the hardware-store clerk what the tiny red flag on the mailbox was for," he recalls with a laugh. Then there was the bat in a bedroom, which they released by opening a window, turning on the light, and stapling a sheet to the door jamb because the house had shifted so much that the door wouldn't close properly. "And the mooing! The sound from the cows up the hill initially terrified us," says Anselmi.

When the couple eventually discovered town, they found themselves in a community teeming with artists, which, on reflection, came as no surprise. "The pace of life here makes you feel comfortable, and when you are comfortable, you can create," says Anselmi. "I think that's why we are here. Because we want to be around people who want a simpler life. We still don't have a dishwasher. And I don't think we ever will."

—————

ABOVE: A classic Cape-style front door, with sidelights and a solid-oak, fan-shaped crown, is painted the color of iron oxide. OPPOSITE: Leavitt's collection of more than a thousand artists' monographs is shelved in a room designed to allow few distractions apart from the Maine light.

PRECEDING PAGES LEFT: To keep all the kitchen's horizontal surfaces at counter height, the couple opted to stash the refrigerator in the pantry.

PRECEDING PAGES RIGHT: "At first, we painted the house in period colors, but it just felt heavy. So we painted it white to make it feel more gallery-like," says Leavitt.

LEFT: The couple paid no mind to the steeply pitched stairs when they first looked at the house; the original banister is a reminder to grab hold going up and down.

BELOW: Classic six-over-six double-hung windows are the defining architectural feature upstairs.

OPPOSITE: One of Leavitt's abstract works hangs over the fireplace.

OPPOSITE: This is a home filled with art and light. Art covers the walls in the hallway leading to the artists' studios.

•

ABOVE AND RIGHT: Sheathed in painted plywood, Leavitt's studio (above) is located in the ell of the house, adjacent to the viewing room (right), where both artists photograph their work and hang it gallery style. A pair of Anselmi's collages and a painting are seen here.

•

OVERLEAF: Works collected over time are hung salon style beneath a stretch of original peg rail.

ROCK CAMP

· · ·

In the world of architecture, there are few absolutes. But one inarguable truth is this: a building is original just once. Expand it, shrink it, reconfigure it, modify it, modernize it, and there's no turning back. Perhaps this was what was swirling around in architect Jocie Dickson's head when she embarked on what could be her most consequential project yet. After all, when your parents are the client, the stakes are high. But Dickson viewed the assignment as a gift; it drew her back to Maine, this time to Portland to live year-round with her husband and their two boys.

Rock Camp sits on a serene, forested lake deep in the southwestern part of the state, where simple, single-story hunting and fishing cabins rim the shore like houses on a Monopoly board. It's a landscape Dickson knows to her core, having spent idyllic childhood summers and winter holidays here with her parents and four siblings. So when she sat down to figure out how to create more sleeping space for the family's ever-expanding brood, she set priorities. "There was always one non-negotiable—I wanted to make the very lightest touch possible on the land, because it's really all about what is outside," says Dickson. Which is why her original idea—to put a second story on the camp structures—never even made it onto paper. "I didn't want to fiddle with the footprint, but I just could not picture the height working in the landscape," she says.

———

Named for the granite boulders strewn about the cove in this particular part of the lake, Rock Camp sits comfortably in the landscape.

Dickson then did what she always does; she stuck to her design philosophy, which puts time and place above all else. "I love the idea of a central lodge for gathering and eating attached to cabins for sleeping, the way my great-grandmother experienced Maine in the 1950s," she says. What she does not embrace is an attempt to make a new building look old. "I feel so strongly about that. Architecture should be true to its time." So she borrowed the original camp's structure and form, repeated it, then wrapped it all in a handful of quiet materials—metal, eastern white cedar (milled in Maine), pine, and glass—to create something original, of this time and of this place. As for adding to its legacy, where her ever-growing extended family gathers every year, Dickson is humbled. "I could talk about the best possible materials and designing things that stand the test of time and all of that, but ultimately, I just want this place to give my boys and their cousins what it gave to my brothers and sisters and me."

———

ABOVE: Sea mist, sunrise, and perhaps a swim?
OPPOSITE: Dickson kept it simple in the additions, using
generous amounts of glass to direct the focus to the outdoors.

OPPOSITE, CLOCKWISE FROM TOP:
A neighboring boathouse is the perfect
size for a Ping-Pong table. There's no
need to see the wall clock constantly; at
Rock Camp, everyone is on Maine time.
Yankee practicality at work: don't post
an intrusive sign when you can get the
message across with a little paint.

•

THIS PAGE,
CLOCKWISE FROM ABOVE LEFT:
Inspired by the great lodges of the early
twentieth century, Dickson wanted to
reserve the original camp for gathering
and create separate spaces for sleeping.
Steel-clad breezeways connect the three
structures. A stick gives an old window a
boost to allow the summer breeze in.

OPPOSITE: Twigs serve as the building material for shelves, a desk, and blanket hooks. ABOVE: The kitchen, tucked under an eave, is fitted out with the essentials, many of which Dickson grew up with.

OVERLEAF: A path leads from the sleeping cottage to the boathouse and the water.

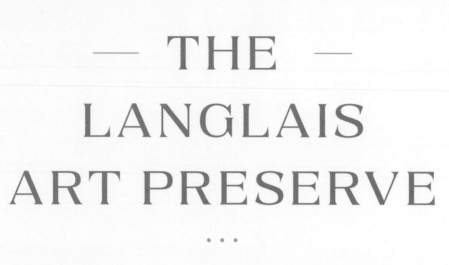

THE — LANGLAIS ART PRESERVE

• • •

In his application for a Guggenheim Fellowship in 1958, Bernard "Blackie" Langlais wrote: "I have long known that I *must paint*; in the past years I have come to know *what* I must paint. To paint in the state of my birth (Maine) and place of my closest association. To be with, and a part of, nature." The artist, who was born in Old Town, had spent the prior two decades studying and making art everywhere from Washington, DC, and the Pacific Islands to New York City, Oslo, and Paris. But Maine? It was his muse, his mistress, and his material source. And the place where he felt most like himself.

Today, the nineteenth-century farmhouse set on ninety acres, where he and his wife, Helen, decided to settle in 1966 and where Langlais began to make the large-scale sculptures that he called his "environmental complex," is an outdoor sculpture preserve stewarded by the

—

Langlais's *Five Bears* lurks behind the barn
in the preserve's sculpture park.

160

Georges River Land Trust, an organization whose mission is to preserve and protect the heritage and ecosystems in the area. It is a baton passed on by Helen, who lived for thirty years on the property after Blackie's death in 1977. "She stayed because it kept Bernard alive for her," says Hannah Blunt, the preserve's director. "I know from people who knew her that she hoped the house and land would become an artist's retreat," she says. And it has. Along with the public sculpture preserve that features more than a dozen of Langlais's larger-than-life pieces, the homestead serves as a place "for making, not just showing," as Helen hoped. She seemed to have shared her husband's belief in the power of place-making, which he so perfectly summed up when describing his desire to be back on his native soil. "I didn't move to Maine to do big things. I did big things because I moved to Maine."

ABOVE: "Nature is my collaborator," Langlais once said.
OPPOSITE: The artist's sculptures express his love of
place through subject and material. He completed *Local
Girl (Christina Olson)*, who lived nearby, in 1968.

OPPOSITE: Langlais, a self-taught carpenter, brought the house back to life to suit him; pieces of colorful cut glass stand in for panes in the door and a tiny pair of carved legs straddle a support beam.

•

THIS PAGE,
CLOCKWISE FROM ABOVE LEFT:
Richard Nixon pops up out of a field in an iconic pose. The artist's spoils: Langlais paid little mind to impermanence. Sculptures in various states of decay surprise on the property.

•

OVERLEAF: Langlais counted Max Beckmann, Edvard Munch, and Piet Mondrian as his mentors and idols. His paintings line the walls of the house.

ABOVE AND RIGHT: A Yankee distaste for waste drove Langlais to recycle everything he could. He worked under the assumption that every wooden scrap that came his way had the potential to find its place in a sculpture or relief.

•

OPPOSITE: Langlais is said to have purchased the home expressly because it had a raised land mass in front, where he eventually mounted his first land sculpture, *Horse*, in 1966, when the area was known for its horse farms.

A GATHERING PLACE

. . .

Tom and Dennie Wolf planted the weeping beech that towers over their bucolic Midcoast property more than a quarter century ago, after a beloved apple tree that once stood there was struck by lightning. Every year, Tom spends a full day with an arborist, pruning, shaping, and supporting the branches, nurturing it as if it were a third child. The visceral pleasures derived from the stewardship of this magnificent specimen, a *Fagus sylvatica*, are obvious. But its care is symbolic too. Both Tom and Dennie have spent the greater part of their lives helping to shape the future of arts and cultural organizations around the world, through the lens of rights, access, and imagination. "This was my family mantra," says Dennie, a fourth-generation Californian, who grew up in a family dedicated to the preservation and health of San Francisco Bay as well as the ranchland around Santa Barbara. Tom, who co-founded the nearby Bay Chamber Concerts & Music School with his brother, Andy, in 1960, descends from one of Russia's most celebrated musicians, the concert violinist Lea Luboshutz, who first visited Maine in 1930 with the Curtis Institute of Music.

The power of everyday imagination is on full display in the Wolfs' late-eighteenth-century home, where Dennie's collections of hooked rugs, quilts, copper pots and pans, and art by Sunday painters hew to a tradition begun by a former owner, Lillian, a sister-in-law of found-object sculptor Louise Nevelson. "It was the mid-1950s, when many small Maine Capes were being modernized to mimic the conveniences of ranch houses. Lillian would drive around in her woodie station wagon and rescue the architectural salvage everyone threw out," says Dennie. "Scavenging and saving are deep in the bones of this house." For some time, what Dennie saw in

---

A view out to the horizon from the screened porch; walking paths gently
carved into the landscape allow for close connection to nature.

her collections—boundless possibility, the impulse to go beyond what is necessary, a sense of life—was not what her husband saw. "Tom would plead with me to stop buying things with rips, chips, and tears." Time—and a hooked-rug expert who deemed several of Dennie's discoveries among the finest she had ever seen—has changed all of that. "I have, over the years, developed a great respect for my wife's eye," says Tom.

For Tom's sprawling extended family—at last count there were fifty-two relatives—the house is their *ur* place. It is where music and art are the shared language, and where Dennie's family mantra—rights, access, and imagination—is always at work. A son-in-law, who is unusually tall and is regularly undone by the kitchen chandelier, perhaps put it best. "This is a family of big tables and small beds."

———

ABOVE: The gathering place of the extended Wolf family.
OPPOSITE: Among the pieces that former owner Lillian rescued was the Good
Morning stair, so called because the occupants of the bedrooms, upon awakening
every day, would face each other and wish each other good morning.

OVERLEAF: "Disparate things teach you something about each of them,
so it is important to combine them, to let them speak," says Dennie.

OPPOSITE: The evidence of the hand is what appeals to Dennie, whether on a copper pot, a braided rug, or a ceramic platter.

ABOVE: An ancient apple tree, one of many on the property, presides over an eighteenth-century stone wall.

RIGHT: The Wolfs acquired the dining room chandelier, made by Deer Isle metalsmith Jack Hemenway, when they were schoolteachers on a nearby Island in 1968.

OVERLEAF: Wood worked by human hands shows up throughout the bedroom: raw planks on the ceiling, hand-hewn pilasters, intricate fretwork on a pair of early-nineteenth-century desks, a planed, sanded, and polished trunk, and a whittled-driftwood music stand.

PAGES 180–81: An alfresco dining area, set beneath a mighty weeping beech, is a perfect spot to watch the sun go down.

PANTHER POND

. . .

There are times when Anne Gass is folding sheets and towels on the bed at the summer camp her great-grandfather built in 1907 that she is overcome. Her mother did this, her grandmother did this, and her great-grandmother did this. In fact, it was here, on this tranquil pond in southern Maine's interior, where that same great-grandmother, Florence Brooks Whitehouse—author, painter, singer, playwright, and suffragette—did some of her deepest thinking. "I'm sitting here in front of the big fire at camp," she wrote to Alice Paul, fellow suffragette and head of the National Women's Party. "It is definitely a place she brought her work," says Gass, author of *Voting Down the Rose: Florence Brooks Whitehouse and Maine's Fight for Woman Suffrage*. In 1919, Maine was the nineteenth state to ratify the 19th Amendment.

That can-do spirit has threaded its way through the generations who have gathered here. Gass's mother and two uncles grew up spending April through October at Panther Pond, then moved to Portland for the winter months. "My parents would switch us into two different school systems every year!" says Gass. That way, her grandfather felt, the family could tend to the Panther Pond garden, which ultimately got them through the Depression. Her mother, who, by the time her twins were born, had six children under the age of seven, encouraged an outdoor life, letting her children spend all day in the woods. "We were a pretty feral bunch," says Gass. She and her siblings take the same approach with the fifteen children among them. "We just figure they will come back to camp when they get hungry," she says with a laugh.

It's hard to imagine a family like this—accomplished activists, politicians, writers, artists, and outdoorsmen among them—taking the time to fuss with the unique

———

When Gass's grandfather was a child, he could reach the tops of the pines
that now tower over the birch- and cedar-shingle-clad log cottage.

design and decoration of this special place. "I've never seen a camp quite like it," says Gass, who professes not to know exactly where the fascination with all that birch came from. "My dad used to complain that it was just a museum. But I don't know how much of it was intention, lack of attention, or lack of funds," she says. What she does maintain, however, is that it will never change. And the expectation is that invited guests will bring their pioneer spirit with them. The fellow who complained about the clogged showerhead (the water is pulled from the pond)? Not invited back. The friend who gleefully recalls the chipmunk who leaped onto the bed while he was reading? Open invitation. And then there was Gass's future son-in-law. He walked into the kitchen and a huge snake slithered across the floor. "He went through with the marriage anyway," she says.

———

ABOVE: Birch beams, benches, bookcases, and chairs are scattered throughout the cottage.
OPPOSITE: The table near the great stone fireplace—which was used for cooking until 1960—has long been the center of activity. In 1917, Florence Brooks Whitehouse used it as her makeshift office.

OVERLEAF: The low, built-in couches have always been irresistible to children for building forts, reading, and socializing. They also serve as extra beds for an overflow of guests.

LEFT: Pleated fabric, affixed to a shelf with upholstery tacks, creates a closet. Gass recalls clambering from room to room over the open rafters as a child.

BELOW: This is a musical family; Gass's grandfather presided over the birch-embellished piano in jam sessions with her two uncles.

OPPOSITE: It's unclear who is responsible for the birch flourishes that show up throughout the cottage, but he or she left a mark in every room.

OVERLEAF: The house sits just seventy-five feet from the water's edge on "one of the best kept secrets in Southern Maine," according to Gass.

ISLAND

OFF
THE GRID,
ON AN ISLAND

...

As a kid, Joe Cutts learned the power of the tides. When catching mackerel off a wharf is the thing you love to do more than anything else, your joy is dictated by the moon's gravitational pull. So it stung whenever his parents dragged him from the mainland out to the tiny island where his grandparents spent the summer living off the grid— no plumbing, heat, or electricity. "I would have to miss a whole high tide to go live like it was the nineteenth century. There was a box of salt cod by the front door. I can still smell it," he says with a laugh.

Decades have passed and Cutts's disdain has turned to devotion. From May to November, he indulges a deep urge—he calls it his life's work—to keep the 1850s cottage that has been in his family for six generations from succumbing to time and Mother Nature. And he resists any intrusion of modern conveniences, all the better to honor his great-great-aunt Josie and her husband, Ivan, who lived here through fierce Maine winters. "She survived him by ten years and couldn't

———

There's no internet here; Cutts's analog island life allows for more music making on a pair of acoustic guitars and a trombone.

195

imagine living anywhere else," says Cutts. To install a bathroom in the house would be heresy. "The sound of plumbing would just ruin it," he says.

His seasonal renters would agree. For the summer months, Cutts turns the cottage over to visitors and decamps to the boathouse Ivan built in 1920. He likes to recall the family who arrived on the island, all pines and jagged shoreline, expecting the broad, sandy beaches of southern Maine. "Even they, by the end of their stay, got the religion," he says.

Cutts, for his part, is devout, mindful of the trade-offs for a life of convenience. Garbage and laundry are a nuisance. And simple summer pleasures are *still* ruled by the ocean's ebb and flow. "My life revolves around high tide. For practical reasons but also because I want to go swimming. That's really why I structure my days around it." But the light. "Just ask the artists. And the dark skies at night. They are black as ink. And it is so quiet. All you can hear is the ringing in your ears and the thrumming of your blood."

———

ABOVE: Cutts lives on an island that has been rendered by artists who have been drawn here since the early 1800s. From the water, passersby can see the property, a vision straight out of a Wyeth painting. OPPOSITE: A view out the front door to the boathouse, where Cutts spends his summers.

OPPOSITE: In summer, meals in the boathouse come with a primo view. ABOVE: The loft in the boathouse is the bedroom, storage room, and an ideal summer reading spot. BELOW: Dinner, if you can catch it, is just out front.

THE
BOAT SHED

. . .

An eighty-foot sloop used to float where Clayton Bright and his wife, Starr, now sit to watch the sunsets that drew his great-grandparents to this mythical part of Maine at the turn of the century. His parents, who made the trip from Philadelphia with their ten children every summer, initially purchased the boathouse with the intention of storing boats, but realized it would better serve as a place to put up their children. "My mother and father used to rent several houses on the island because it was difficult to stuff us all into one place," says Bright. Accommodations varied according to what was available. One summer, they rented a defunct hotel with just the right number of rooms. "The hidden treasure was a cookbook for quantity cooking. I will never forget the chocolate pudding. And I am talking a big pot of pudding," he says.

The sprawling Bright family traveled north by train until the mid-1950s, when service to nearby Ellsworth ended. "It was the best way, because we'd sleep in the overhead luggage racks," says Bright. A chartered bus was the next most efficient option. "The bus would come to the house, and we would load our various pets and bicycles onto it and go to Maine," he says. Bright's Maine was a car-free island where he and his three brothers and six sisters roamed free and rode those bicycles fearlessly, where independence came young and community mattered. "In a short walk, you would have three conversations with other islanders," he says.

Bright installed an interior glass wall along the front of the boathouse to create
a porch as well as to preserve the architectural integrity of the structure.

Those were the kind of summers the couple wanted for their three children. To that end, Bright designed bedrooms in the boathouse strictly for sleeping; each features two twin beds, a built-in bureau, a closet, and a bookcase. "We didn't want them hiding out in their rooms when all the action was outside." He also aimed to foster the sense of community that compelled him so much as a child. "I grew up in houses where the kitchen was always separate from the public rooms, but here, I wanted something more convivial." He took inspiration from the curved deck houses on the schooners that sail along the coast.

Though grown now, the Bright children never miss a summer in this idyllic place, falling effortlessly into the rhythms of island life with their dozens of cousins and aunts and uncles and island friends. As for the senior Bright, that is what it is all about. "Topeka is probably a nice place if you live there and know the people. I ended up on an island in Maine and got to know the people. And they make it everything."

———

OPPOSITE: A picture window, boathouse style. ABOVE: The boathouse doors are opened in May and remain so until the weather demands that the pipes be drained and the windows boarded up.

ABOVE: The spruce-clad kitchen is inspired by curved deck houses on schooners. "I just drew a curved line to separate the kitchen and living room because there are too many 90-degree angles in this house," says Bright. BELOW: Of the nine boathouses on Bright's "street," two remain boathouses and one is an artist's studio. OPPOSITE: Bright designed the great room to take advantage of the light, which draws everyone to it; no warren of tiny rooms here. OVERLEAF: The sun sets over Acadia National Park.

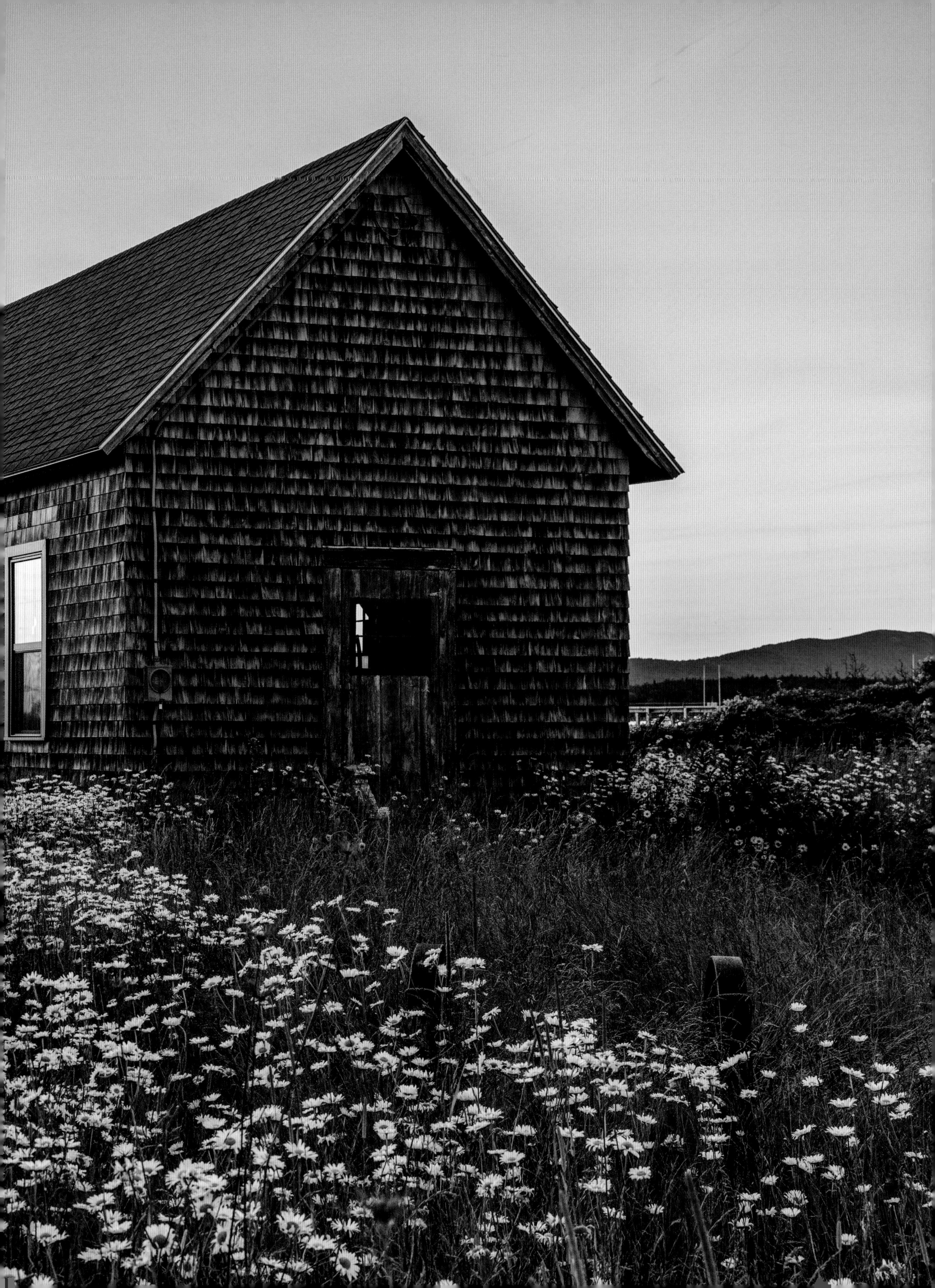

THE WOODLAWN HOUSE

. . .

Of the almost 4,000 islands in Maine, just 300 were ultimately settled, and of those, 100 eventually became year-round communities, a number that has dwindled to just 15 today. "A place is always richer when families are being raised there," says John Fondas, who knows something about island living. Born and raised in Spanish Wells in the Bahamas, he hadn't connected with any place quite like it until he stepped onto Little Cranberry Island's public dock more than two decades ago. "The lobster traps, the gardens, the lobstermen's co-op, it all reminded me of home," he says.

The Woodlawn Inn was in terrible shape, but its history—and history-making view—captivated Fondas and his partner, John Knott. From the front porch, one can see Bunker's Ledge, where Frederic Church made *Beacon Off Mount Desert Island*, the painting that put Maine on the map as a tourist destination in the late 1800s. The inn's nineteen tiny bedrooms drew notable painters—Mary Cassatt among them—as well as the era's rusticators, who made the trip from Boston, Philadelphia, and New York City. "We meticulously preserved the exterior and took only a few liberties with the interior architecture to make it more relaxed and open," says Fondas of the gambrel-roofed Colonial Revival. Hints at the house's former life are everywhere—the linoleum stair runner, the room numbers, the exit signs all remain.

And then they went to town. Or, rather, to sea. Like a pair of New England sea captains, they furnished the house with exotica that might have been brought back from excursions to the Far East. But Fondas and Knott, mindful that the best old vacation houses are those in which a motley mix of family cast-offs land, looked no further than their own cache; all of the furnishings came out of homes they had owned

A collection of late nineteenth-century landscapes
of Nova Scotia, collected over time, hangs in the hallway.

in the past. "It's that grand recycling that makes these houses so idiosyncratic. They're filled with bits and pieces of people's lives," says Fondas. For this pair, the principals of the textile company Quadrille, that includes miles of fabric and wallcoverings deployed with joyful abandon—just the way they like it.

Which is why, when summer rolls around and the sheets come off the furniture, the shutters are opened, and the pipes come to life, Fondas is content to stay right here. "I don't want to be dancing on some Mediterranean island. I want to smell the soil, listen to the loons, and share the view with our friends," he says. The rewards of island living, he finds, far outweigh the inconveniences. "You actually appreciate your bottle of water, your screwdriver, and your ballpoint pen."

———

OPPOSITE: Etched in Greek into the lintel over the Colonial Revival's front door: "The sea shall wash away the ills of man." ABOVE: A view of Bunker's Ledge, made famous by nineteenth-century painter Frederic Church.

OVERLEAF: The house is filled with what Fondas calls a "very American mixture of different furniture styles, family hand-me-downs, and the kind of China trade exotica that New England sea captains collected."

OPPOSITE: The hallway wallpaper is based on a nineteenth-century French document that the couple found on their travels. ABOVE: A Maine tableau: the nautical chart and cherry drop-leaf table both hail from the Pine Tree State.

OVERLEAF LEFT: Fondas and Knott filled the house with pieces from a previous home: a silver hotel punch bowl set on a tramp art table glistens in the sunlight.
OVERLEAF RIGHT: All of the original doors remain, as do the room numbers.

PRECEDING PAGES: "We have a love of birdcages and a love of birds, but no birds in cages," says Fondas.

•

OPPOSITE: As an homage to the founding of America, a guest room is swathed in Independence toile, featuring Franklin, Washington, and Lady Liberty.

•

THIS PAGE,
CLOCKWISE FROM ABOVE LEFT:
An antique taxidermy lobster, lovingly referred to as "Mr. Claw," hangs next to a surrealist seascape by island artist Dan Fernald. The chest of drawers is original to the house. In a guest bedroom, antique watercolors of birds embellished with real feathers adorn the walls.

HARBOR
LIGHTS

. . .

Memorial Day weekend is a big one at Harbor Lights, a Shingle Style seaside cottage in southern Maine that has been in this family for five generations. "It's the same every year," says Emily Appleton, whose great-great-grandparents purchased the place a decade after it was built in 1910. "The image of my mother teetering on the back of the sofa trying to get the curtain rods in place will stay with me forever." When she was a child, Appleton's summer officially started the day school ended, with the station wagon packed that morning. "My parents picked my sister and me up as soon as the bell rang and got us to use the bathroom at school because there was no stopping between Massachusetts and the house," she says. They were only outdone by friends in a cottage nearby. "They would buy all of their school supplies in Wells, and leave at 5 a.m. on the day school started in September."

Highlights of Appleton's summers span the arc of her life—boogie boarding at age two, spending all day in the tidal pools as a toddler, swimming until her lips turned blue as a kid, stealing an ancient bottle of Southern Comfort from a high shelf in the kitchen as a teenager, and watching from the porch as Hurricane Bill kicked up monstrous waves as a young adult. It is the rituals around arriving and leaving,

---

The seasonal opening and closing of the cottage is a cherished
ritual, as familiar as the tides, for the Appleton family,
who have been coming here for five generations.

however, that elicit the deepest nostalgia; the to-do lists read largely, and comfortingly, as they always have. As time passes, and the beach just beyond the front porch continues its dramatic shift (Appleton has fond memories of walks to an estuary at high tide, now impassable), the constancy of what appears to be a banal rundown of chores—drape Bea's desk with a sheet, remove liquids from pantry, especially vinegar and salsa, remove foods that mice like, pull utensil drawer out and place on gas stove, then cover with nun painting, put away surfboards and wet suits, close the shutters, bring in the full window screens that can blow away, fold blankets and quilts inside out and cover with mattress cover, hang an older sheet over pantry dishes, take home paint, telescope, liquor—is for Appleton a steadying rite, assurance that in a world filled with unpredictability, there is one place she can count on to be reliably, beautifully the same.

———

ABOVE: When your house faces the Atlantic, storm doors are the great
protectors, assuring that the paned doors will be there next summer.
OPPOSITE: The summer sound of a slamming screen door is silenced all winter,
having been taken off its hinges and leaned against a wall just inside the front door.

OPPOSITE: Every year, the piece atop the chest of drawers is covered with a sheet anchored by a collection of mugs. ABOVE: It is perhaps the only time stillness pervades this ancestral summer house, yet winter brings with it a beautiful silence. BELOW: "Bring in the full window screens that can blow away—including the bathroom one," reads the Harbor Lights closing list. OVERLEAF: Little is more gratifying than swiping the sheets from the furniture to let the summer begin.

KILLICK

· · ·

"I have always thought it was pretentious to name a house," says Jack Partridge, who has spent all but his first two summers in the Craftsman-inspired cottage his parents purchased more than seventy-five years ago. The handsome shingled house, at the mouth of the harbor on a car-free Midcoast island, is now humbly referred to as the Partridge place, yet its original name seems a fitting metaphor for this extended family of more than thirty. A killick—a primitive anchor fashioned from a stone caged in a stick frame—is used to moor small boats; for this far-flung family, it defines the place that grounds them more than anywhere else in the world.

"It is the only constant in my life," says Jessie Partridge, Jack's daughter with wife, Miki. "We moved around a bunch and this house, this island, my favorite diving rock, going barefoot to get my summer feet, the sleeping hammock in the dorm room, are the things I dream about all year long," she says. Which is why, when she was set to marry Edwin Guerrero, there was never any question where the ceremony would take place. Not even the tail end of Hurricane Harvey could unmoor them. They hung an elaborate garland on the great room mantel and said their vows by the fireplace in front of 120 friends and family members.

Little has changed since Killick was built by an islander in 1908, when oxen carried lumber up to the bluff from the dock. Most of the furniture came with the house, and it wasn't until 2001 that the family agreed to run electricity through the place. Though Jack carries around a list of possible

---

Well over a hundred years of sunsets have awed all who have
stepped onto the northwest-facing porch, built with wood carried
up the hill from the dock by oxen in the early 1900s.

upgrades in his shirt pocket, he is mindful that the replacement of the gas lights that illu-
minated the great room and kitchen just five years ago felt like an act of betrayal—and ever
closer to their onshore lives. "I was so worried that no longer having to live by lanterns and
candlelight would take the magic out of the place," says Jessie.

But it hasn't. In fact, Miki has been known to stay in the house long after the fireplace
can adequately warm her. "I stayed for a month one winter and needed to wear spikes to
walk anywhere outside," she says. "It's isolating in the most beautiful way." A dishwasher
and a bidet are on Jack's list, and Jessie votes for new mattresses, all to be discussed over
and over and over. But there is one thing that will never ever change at Killick. "It has kept
our extended family connected in a world where it is so easy to be anything but," says Jack.

ABOVE: An iconic Maine scene, viewed through the living room window. OPPOSITE: "I guess
it's sort of woven into my life, so much a part of what I have always known—the friendships
here, the longtime visitors who still come. Plus, it's just a beautiful place and we have this
beautiful house and most of us still find it special. It's part of my DNA," says Jack Partridge.

OVERLEAF: Most of the furniture came with the house—and is
still pressed into service when the house is full.

OPPOSITE: According to family lore, the carved schooner over the fireplace depicts Captain John Smith rounding the point of the tiny island known as Smutty Nose, visible from the house. ABOVE: The recently installed electric lights that replaced gas-powered versions flank the front door, a Dutch version with a bull's-eye glass porthole that allows the salt air and Maine light to flow through the house.

LEFT: Yankee ingenuity is on display in the stairway, where built-in drawers make use of often overlooked space.

•

BELOW: Very little has been added to the kitchen shelves since Jack was a toddler; the family has been eating off of the same plates for decades.

•

OPPOSITE: Miki's preferred spot is on the built-in, fifteen-foot-long bench that looks out onto the neighboring island. "I can sit and read there for hours," she says.

ABOVE: An awning window can
stay open all summer; it lets the salt
air in and keeps the rain out.

LEFT: A built-in window seat offers a
bird's-eye view of the harbor below.

OPPOSITE: A swinging hammock hangs
in front of an ocean-facing window in
the dorm room. Cotton ropes, slung
between the rafters, serve as clotheslines
for wet towels and bathing suits.

OVERLEAF: The view of the
island across the channel from
the bedroom window seat.

AN ARTIST'S EDEN

. . .

"I find it immensely gratifying to use stuff up. I love figuring out what to do when I get to the end of something. A ballpoint pen, Chapstick—I'll find a use for it," says artist Sam Shaw. He calls the Ten Spot, the decagonal folly he built on a forested plot on the "wrong side" of a tiny island, the most extreme example of his desire to use and save everything. It is just one of a cluster of structures that the sculptor and jeweler has erected in his self-described fantasy world, where the distractions of day-to-day living—Wi-Fi, mail, books, magazines, television—do not exist. Designed strictly for the warmer months, the Ten Spot, the Naughtyless, the Crystal Palace, the Blunt House, the Laboratory, and the Shipwright give Shaw a chance to experiment. "In Maine, you have to build largely with practicality in mind, but in the summer you get to be a bit silly," he says. About reuse, however, the man is dead serious.

It was at a proverbial fork—his graduation from college—that Shaw chose to return to the place where generations of his family had spent their summers. "You move somewhere for either work or beauty. For me there was no choice. I picked the most beautiful place I had ever known," he says. In the four decades since, Shaw's mission has been to amplify nature's aesthetic by reinterpreting it—he was an early adapter of beachstone jewelry—and using what is available to him. "These buildings are of the land, but through my eyes," he says.

The Blunt House, a shrine to Shaw's deceased daughter, is a storage space built from logs and decommissioned sails. "It's a working shed now, filled with sculptures and detritus. She would have liked that. She was a bit of a mess maker and an artist herself," he says. The Crystal Palace was born out of a change of heart. Shaw's original vision for the Naughtyless was one entirely built from windows. "But then I changed my mind and had to figure out what to do with a hundred of them," he says. It became obvious when

---

Shaw brought a hundred windows out to the property to use in the Naughtyless (see pages 252–53) but changed his mind, so he used them to build the Crystal Palace between four trees that form a perfect rectangle.

he espied four stick-straight trees in a perfect rectangle, nature's gift by way of a footprint. Of the Naughtyless, Shaw describes an obsession with the form and its reference to infinity, a concept he struggles to embrace. The challenge of laying its foundation dogged him until, after building model after model, he had the aha moment. "The answer was to build forty-four posts angled in a pattern like spokes on a wheel," he says.

Shaw describes his buildings as pearls and the paths connecting them as the string. He is inclined to cull the plants that line them rather than impose on them. "What's easiest to grow is already here, so rather than plant things, I just let the land do what it wants and get out of the way." Indeed, Shaw sees his role here as a steward whose sole purpose is to continually create beauty. "I don't think about function because that can change. This place will outlive me, and someone else will come along and have a completely different idea. How it is used is far less important to me than the pleasure I get from making it."

———

ABOVE: Shaw set out to erect just one building on the property, beginning in 2004. Today, there are close to ten, with several more in various states of completion. OPPOSITE: Shaw acquired the doors to the Naughtyless (see pages 252–53), which are covered in markings that could be Chinese seals, at an auction on a tip from a friend. "I suspect the metal fittings are there to dull uninvited guests' axes," he says.

OPPOSITE: Shaw made more than ten
models before he figured out how to
build the Naughtyless, the spiral-shaped
wonder whose form references infinity.

•

THIS PAGE,
CLOCKWISE FROM ABOVE LEFT:
Shaw's lightbulb moment for construction of
the Naughtyless was to build forty-four posts
angled in a pattern like the spokes of a wheel.
He likes to say that he lives on the "wrong" side
of the island, where the Atlantic has created a
stone beach. Shoe anvils make useful handles
on the doors to the Laboratory, Shaw's studio.

•

OVERLEAF: The Blunt House, a
storage shed built from old sails, is a
shrine to Shaw's daughter, who passed
away at twenty-nine years old.

ABOVE: A pair of towering pines provides the armature for a door that marks the line between a mature forest and new growth, as well as the transition from the sea side of the property to the home side. "We ask people to knock first, and to close it quickly so as not to let the mosquitoes in," says Shaw. "Just to be silly." OPPOSITE: The roof of Shaw's studio, the Laboratory, riffs on Asian architecture. Designed to mimic slate, it is made of recycled rubber from old tires.

CAPTAIN JOHN'S CAMP

. . .

Next to nothing is known about how John Reilly made his way from Mexico, Texas, to this Midcoast Maine island, but legend has it that he spent part of his life riding the rails, tossing vagrants out of train cars. One can only imagine, then, that the scrappy Reilly, a reclusive lobsterman known to islanders as Captain John, must have arrived here and headed straight to the salvage yard, where he nicked the boards to build a two-room shack in which to live. He eventually added a workshop for repairing traps and repainting buoys, which he did until the last year of his life, when the Dorr family, whose island ties run deep, cared for him until the day he died.

Perhaps sensing in them kindred spirits, Reilly passed on the camp to his caretakers, and they have been honoring its ethos ever since. Three generations of Dorrs have made their mark on the place, largely through additions—the kitchen and dining area, followed by the tower—and, not surprisingly, few subtractions (an interior wall here and there). Every bit of it was fashioned and furnished through trips to the transfer station and the swap shop. "It was all in the free flow of goods. And that includes the stereo system," says Greg Dorr, who inculcated the scavenger spirit in his son Ben, now the proprietor of a vintage-clothing consignment shop on the mainland. "Most things deserve a much longer life than we give them," Ben says.

To that end, the Dorrs have filled the diminutive camp from floor to ceiling with found and handmade objects, each seeming to have

---

"We love to find the thing that has been cast aside, yet still has life in it, and make it desirable again. It has always been part of our family life," says Ben Dorr.

a heartbeat all its own. To walk through the door is to step into a life-size cabinet of curiosities. "A couple of years ago, a friend hung a few things on the wall and wouldn't tell us where. They fit in so perfectly we still can't find them," says Ben.

Chances are other guests have left mementos behind too. In his younger days, Ben's costume parties—all the clothing was found—at the camp were legendary, with friends making their way out to the island from all over the Midcoast. "There are no cops here," he says. That generosity of spirit—and the excitement that comes from sharing this place—lives on in the Dorr family. A few summers ago, Ben discovered that a couple browsing in his shop had just eloped, so he sent them out to the camp for a few nights. "It's so gratifying to share that world," he says. But still, he's protective. The newlyweds, taken with their benefactor's kindness, couldn't believe such a community existed. "I jokingly said to them, 'Don't tell anyone when you get home.'"

_____

ABOVE: The exterior may appear unassuming, but step inside the Dorr camp and that assumption is turned on its head. OPPOSITE: Maps are collected for both their utility and beauty.

OVERLEAF: The aesthetic is a mix of the elder Dorr's taste in art and his endless talent for seeing beauty in what others toss out. "It's all about the context in which you put it," says Ben.

ABOVE: A rescued door turned on
its side and a window frame separate
the kitchen from the living room.

•

LEFT: No fuzzy slippers here: a
pair of sunny yellow babouches
are the house shoes of choice.

•

OPPOSITE: The complete
works of Shakespeare line a
shelf in the bedroom.

THE OMP

· · ·

"I love the challenge of a beautiful old house," says Brian Woods. The historic preservationist, design/builder, and artist has had a passion for old houses ever since he was a kid. At twenty-three and newly married, he and his wife, Nancy, restored an 1880s farmhouse in Vermont's Northeast Kingdom, only to lose it to a fire—from a lightning strike—just as their work was done. It burned to the ground. Their next project was a two-story Federal in the woods of central Vermont, with draft horses and a maple-sugaring operation. After that, they restored and settled into a 1790s Cape back in the Northeast Kingdom, where they lived for the next forty years.

Why, one might wonder, would the Woodses trade their beloved Green Mountain State for the coast of Maine? "Vermont has the best politics in the nation, but it doesn't have the ocean," says Brian. And, well, the couple found another challenge in another beautiful old house—this one on a tiny Midcoast island that cherishes what it does not have: cars, power lines, and plumbing. Which might explain why the Woodses are just the second owners of the OMP (Old Maids' Paradise), a loosely interpreted Greek Revival built in 1850 by James Simmons, who is buried in the cemetery on the island. Named for his three daughters, who lived together in the house well into middle age, the OMP is one of eight similar homesteads—along with thirty small cottages—whose footprint here is featherlight.

———

Woods's aim was to keep the house as sparse as possible. "I just love the idea of the simplicity of plaster walls with no adornment."

"There is a purity about this place," says Woods. It is an ethos he clung to as the couple peeled away 150 years of "improvements." "'Preservationists are always relieved when a well-built home has been inhabited by people of little means; they cover up instead of tear out the original bones of a house," he says. To his surprise, all of the original doors and hardware were right where they had always been, and underneath a half-dozen layers of linoleum lay the original pine floors. Woods kept it sparse—simple plaster walls and no adornments—to honor the original character of the place. And, perhaps, to conjure a bit of what Thoreau was looking to do when he retreated to the woods: "to live so sturdily and Spartan-like as to rout all that was not life, to cut a broad swath and shave close, to drive life into a corner, and reduce it to its lowest terms."

———

OPPOSITE: The pump organ is one of five on this small island, either the result of a peddler's efforts or ordered through a catalog. ABOVE: Under layers of linoleum, water-soaked wallpaper, and broken windows was an arrestingly simple kitchen.

OVERLEAF: Woods has been attracted to the simplicity of Shaker furniture since he was a teenager. Antiques with a local provenance—vintage wooden buoys, a wooden ironing board, a blueberry rake, and a bare blanket rack—reflect his less-is-more approach.

OPPOSITE: Against an all-white backdrop, furniture reads as sculpture.

•

RIGHT AND ABOVE LEFT: Woods prefers painted floors, owing to his background in historic preservation.

•

ABOVE RIGHT: Woods spent a decade bringing the Greek Revival, one of eight original homesteads on the island, back to life.

THE LIGHTHOUSE

. . .

"What's more unique than living in a lighthouse?" Jamie Wyeth asks the question rhetorically because he clearly knows the answer. In Wyeth's world, nowhere on the planet comes close to feeding body, mind, and soul the way home on a Midcoast island does. "It's like running away with the circus," he says. Or, in his case, with just the animals. And that is exactly the way Wyeth likes it. As a boy, he left school to be tutored at home, where most of his companions hailed from the natural world. "It's as simple as that. I knew more animals than people."

But people knew *him*. When your branch on the family tree descends from N. C. and Andrew Wyeth, two of America's most beloved artists, solitude can be hard won. But Wyeth insists on it. "I like to go to the theater and to concerts like anyone else, but there is a certain deprivation about living on an island that I love. That sense of isolation—and when there is so little—is when I work best," he says. That philosophy extends to his wardrobe, tall rain boots into which he stuffs his pants, which are cut off at the knee to make the stuffing easier. Those pants, morphed into proper knickers,

---

"I thought living on an island would be like
living on a boat. Islands intrigue me. You can see the
perimeters of your world." —Jamie Wyeth

along with a turtleneck and sometimes a button-up vest, constitute his attire. "I jump out of bed and into my uniform. Because the only eyes on me are the seagulls'," he says.

Of course, when he took up residence here, he wondered how he would live and work in what looks like an Andrew Wyeth painting. "My father pretty much painted it all. I thought maybe I'd paint the bugs," he says with a laugh. But after a few years, the artist began to see so much more. "I could live four lifetimes and not scratch the surface of what this place offers up to me every single day," he says. "The lighthouse itself is a symbol and so singular. It's like a person." One that expands his perspective every day. "There is something about the view from the top of the lighthouse, seeing the perimeter of the world, that is just thrilling," says Wyeth. But it is those closest to home—the seagulls—that have had the greatest impact on this painter. "I've drawn them so much that they fall asleep next to me. They think I am one of them. And sometimes, I think I am too."

OPPOSITE: The stained interior of a corner cabinet filled with transferware suggests a traditional nautical palette. ABOVE: *The Rakish Brigantine Sea Captain in the Storm* by Wyeth's grandfather N. C. Wyeth looks after him in his bedroom.

OPPOSITE: There is always a dry pair of boots ready for the artist to jump into; wet boots are treated to Wyeth's unique method for drying them out. ABOVE: Weather shapes much of Wyeth's life on the island and with it, a fascination with weather-related instruments like the pair of sculptural antique lightning rods.

OVERLEAF: "I collect things purely with an eye to painting them or at least to getting a feeling for them while I work. I'm not a true collector," says Wyeth.

ABOVE: Wyeth works best with little stimulation. "I don't need lots of people around. And I paint pretty much constantly. The opium for me is when things start clicking—when the portrait of a seagull or a tree finally comes alive." OPPOSITE: For an islander, cooking is self-preservation. "The fishermen drop things off at the end of my float, and I grow vegetables in my garden. You can't just pop out to the grocery store. You make do with what you have on hand," says Wyeth.

OVERLEAF: When the ocean surrounds you, two viewing scopes are better than one.

ABOVE: "The sea is right there, and that is the attraction," says Wyeth. OPPOSITE: Antique dioramas of schooners line an oxidized, double-beadboard wall in a bathroom.

OVERLEAF: Sunrise on the island.

For my parents, Al and Maureen, who tirelessly made Maine our place.

M.M.

•

*To my Mainer parents, Judith and Brian, who went "away" for a while
but came home determined to raise their children in Maine. You gave
me the courage, skills, and DIY spirit to take on Reach Winds.*

B.B.

•

For Stephen, Finn, and James, who make any *house a home.*

K.H.

ACKNOWLEDGMENTS

There is so much thought that goes into a book like this. Foremost is a desire to leave something good in my wake, something to pass down to the next generation, be it a book or a house. That means especially, emphatically, to my daughter, Oona, and ideally to generations beyond, in whatever form they may take. —M.M.

Thank you, Nana Dede, Grampy Bill, and the entire Foster family, who taught me what family—and sharing a summer cottage—is all about. —B.B.

My first teachers were my mother and father, who instilled in me an appreciation for beauty, gave me the gift of pragmatism, and modeled what it means to live a spirited life. Thank you from the bottom of my heart. And of course, my Maine family, the Youngs, without whom life would be far less sweet and humorous. —K.H.

And from the three of us:

Thank you, first and foremost, to the people of Maine.

We can hardly call it a job, this endeavor to create a record of Maine's particular architectural beauty, because it is where our hearts largely live. To be able to motor, ferry, and row to "work" made the business of capturing the heart and soul of these homes and their owners as pleasurable as it gets. Driving the rural roads of Maine means being in a continuous state of awe and wonder, not to mention discipline; if we had stopped every time we spotted a glorious farmhouse, church, Oddfellows hall, ice fisherman, farmstand, and breathtaking vista, we never would have made our scheduled rounds.

And the rounds we made! So many of you hosted these three perfect strangers, fed us, ferried us, toasted us, entertained us, regaled us, and just gave so much of your time. A heartfelt thank-you to you all. Drew Hodges, John Fondas and John Knott, Scott and Martha Finlay, Jocie Dickson, Jamie Wyeth, Sarah Webb, Sharon and Paul Mrozinski, and the Madara family opened their doors and offered up accommodations—during the summer!—when beds are at a premium. We couldn't have done it without you. A big thank-you to Joe Cutts, Susan Beebe, Scott and Martha Finlay, Emmy Lewis, and Brendan Chase for hopping in your boats to motor us from dock to dock, some of you rising cruelly early in the spirit of capturing Maine at its finest hour. And to adequately tell Emily Muir's architectural story, a thank-you to Kam Mitchell for the use of his drone. To those of you who shared the secret hiding spot for your keys, entrusted your special camps, cottages, and homes to us, and so enthusiastically shared your stories, we could not be more grateful.

Making books is not for the faint of heart and to that end, there are a bevy of professionals, largely unsung, who are pivotal along its lifespan. Carla Glasser is the best agent, as we pointed out in our previous book. That sentiment remains. To our friends at Vendome, who are among our biggest cheerleaders—publisher Mark Magowan, Nina Magowan, editor Jackie Decter, designer Mark Melnick, production director Jim Spivey, and publicist Meghan Phillips—a very big thank-you. We are so very proud to publish with you.

Lastly, but perhaps most importantly, thank you to the booksellers of all stripes for making room for us (and hopefully shelved face out!). Your enthusiasm for our previous book made a difference and is so crucial to our ongoing mission to encourage preservation, restoration, and sensitive building practices in this great state. It's a pursuit worth supporting.

THE MAINE HOUSE II

First published in 2024 by The Vendome Press

Vendome is a registered trademark of The Vendome Press, LLC

VENDOME PRESS US	VENDOME PRESS UK
P.O. Box 566	Worlds End Studio
Palm Beach, FL 33480	132-134 Lots Road
	London, SW10 0RJ

www.vendomepress.com

Distributed by Abrams Books

ISBN 978-0-86565-442-6

Publishers: Beatrice Vincenzini, Mark Magowan, and Francesco Venturi
Editor: Jacqueline Decter
Production Director: Jim Spivey
Designer: Mark Melnick

Library of Congress Cataloging-in-Publication Data
available upon request

Printed and bound in China by 1010 Printing International Ltd.

First printing

———

FRONT ENDPAPERS: A prized collection of heirloom books and treasures line the walls of a family cottage on Mount Desert Island.

PAGE 1: A photograph of the Foster family's cottage (see pages 22–31) hangs between a pair of windows dressed as
they always have been—in country curtains chosen to match the American pine hobnail bedspread.

PAGES 2–3: The saltwater farm where Drew Hodges and Peter Kukielski, an expert on disease resistance
in rose gardens, replaced the lawn with sustainable creeping thyme (see pages 84–95).

PAGES 4–5: An idiosyncratic mix of windows reflects the sunset that the Partridge family
enjoys from their porch most summer evenings (see pages 234–47).

PAGES 6–7: A century-old island house, wrapped in cedar shakes, shingles, and siding,
speaks nature's language, right down to the moss-covered clothesline.

PAGES 8–9: The morning view from Rock Camp (see pages 150–59), where sea fog and mountains meet.

PAGES 10–11: Monhegan Island.

PAGE 294: The view of Manana Island from Monhegan Island.

FRONT OF BACK ENDPAPERS: The Maine House mantra, taped to the Young family's window casing.

BACK ENDPAPERS: Spruce, apple, or birch? An artful woodpile offers up them all.

Old buildings
can be used

recent letter